Symbols of Christ

BY

DAMASUS WINZEN, O. S. B.

MONK OF MARIA LAACH

Drawings by

WILLIAM V. CLADEK

Volume I: The Old Testament

KEYPORT, NEW JERSEY

1944

Imprimi potest
Die 5a Julii 1944

✠ Patritius M. O'Brien
Abbas B.M. Immaculatae Novarcensis

Imprimatur
Die 5a Julii 1944

✠ Gulielmus Aloysius Griffin, D.D.
Episcopus Trentonensis

Introduction

—

The word "symbol" is derived from the Greek "symballein" which means "to piece together." It was a wide-spread custom in the antiquity that the host broke a potsherd or a ring and gave one half to his guest, retaining the other half. When the guest came back, the one half of the potsherd fitting into the other proved him a guest with the right of hospitality. The "symbol" made him at home.

God has created this visible world as a "symbol," as the one half of the potsherd; His Divine Wisdom, which was with Him as His master workman when He marked the foundations of the earth, being the other half. Then God created man and breathed His Spirit into him that he should fit the world to God's Wisdom and thus prove himself at home in God's house. "The wheel of creation revolves with a circumference embracing all that man's eye can reach, and he stands as the centre of the circle, the visible god of this lower world" (Herder, *The Spirit of Hebrew Poetry*, tr. by J. Marsh, vol. II, p. 7). In searching out the essence of things, giving names to all and praising God in His works, man was a priest officiating in the temple of this world. But when he yielded to the temptation of the serpent and wanted to be wiser than God, "his eyes were opened," as it is said sarcastically in Holy Scripture (*Genesis* 3, 7) and he saw, not God, but himself, his own flesh. "God has made everything beautiful in its time. He has set the world into man's heart, yet man cannot find out the work that God has done from the beginning even to the end" (*Ecclesiastes* 3, 11). Man had lost the "symbol." He had lost his home. From now on he lived as an exile, not as a guest, in this world.

To protect the secrets of His heart from the profane ears and eyes of an unholy generation, God concealed His Wisdom in the signs and parables of the Old Testament. "Hearing they hear and understand not: and see visions and know it not. Blind the heart of this people and make their ears heavy and shut their eyes: lest they see with their eyes and hear with their ears, and understand with their heart, and be converted and I heal them" (*Isaias* 6, 9/10). After a long time of speaking in parables and uttering dark sayings (*Ps.* 77, 2) Christ came, and after His resurrection He "opened their understanding, that they might understand the Scriptures" (*Luke* 25, 45). In other words, He gave to His disciples, to all those who are reborn in the water and the Holy Spirit, the Old Testament as their "symbol" that they may fit it to the Divine Wisdom incarnate, crucified and risen, and thus prove themselves to be at home in the house of the Father of Jesus Christ. In Pentecost God set the Old Testament into the hearts of the faithful as He once had set the word into man's heart when He breathed His spirit into him at the beginning of history.

That it may not be said again: "Yet the faithful cannot find out the work that God has done from the beginning even to the end," the following pages are written. They try to give a strictly scriptural interpretation of those symbols of the Old Testament which refer to the Messiah. From the texts given underneath each symbol the reader can easily see how these symbols of the Messiah are like red threads which go through the whole of the two Testaments and knit them together into a marvellous unity. The explanation on the facing page tries to show the harmony between the natural and the scriptural meaning of the symbol. Christ really is the "recapitulation" of the universe. In Him all things have found their head.

But, at the same time, the symbols of the Old Testament differ essentially from the mere cosmic symbolism of any pagan religion. To pagan thinking symbols like the sun or the tree are embodiments of the healing powers inherent in nature. They never point to a *Saviour* who, through his personal sacrificial love heals the wounds of human guilt and restores an order which had been destroyed by sin. Symbols like the Burning Bush and the Brazen Serpent, which foreshadow the incarnation and the crucifixion, have no parallel in pagan symbolism. Symbols which are universal, as the tree, the cross, the mountain, the sun, etc., receive in Holy Scripture a new significance, over and above their "natural" meaning, which points to the work of redemption. Especially the glory of the resurrection radiates from each one of the Old Testament symbols. This is not surprising when we consider that the meaning of a symbol in ancient times was not so much the conveying of an idea to the mind than the communication of life to the whole being of man. The cross, for example, never was an illustration of an abstract truth, but a sign, a "sacramental" which represents and causes the "wholeness" of life. This "sacramental" character of the cross remains in the Christian use of the symbol, but now it derives its healing power from the fact that it represents the lifegiving death of Christ.

All the symbols explained in these pages represent the *fullness* of the salvation wrought by Christ. They are not limited to one aspect of Christ's work. They comprehend the whole history of redemption, uniting the beginning and the end (*cf.* the Rod of Jesse, etc.). They embrace death and life (for example, the Brazen Serpent). They express the mystical identity between Christ and His people (for example, the Holy Mountain, the Corner Stone).

To contemplate them is, therefore, a preparation for that blissful vision in which we shall some time see all things in God's Word.

The Seal of the Living God

"And the Lord set a mark upon Cain, that whosoever found him should not kill him." (*Genesis* 4, 15).

"And the Lord said: Go through the midst of Jerusalem and mark Taw upon the foreheads of the men that sigh, and mourn for all the abominations that are committed in the midst thereof." (*Ezechiel* 9, 4).

"And I saw another angel ascending from the rising of the sun, having the seal of the living God, and he cried with a loud voice to the four angels to whom it was given to harm the earth and the sea, saying: Do not harm the earth, or the sea, or the trees, till we have sealed the slaves of our God on their foreheads."

(*Apoc.* 7, 2/3).

THE SEAL OF THE LIVING GOD

LONG before Our Lord was crucified the cross was a sign sacred to men. The integrity and stability of the universe seems to rest on the cross. It points into the four directions of the compass. All living beings are shaped in the pattern of a cross. Spreading their wings in the form of a cross the birds master the air. In the power of their cruciform masts the boats cross the waves. The cross brings firmness to walls and fences and buildings. No wonder that it appeared as a sign of salvation in the earliest days of human history. It was used as a brand for animals and slaves. The illiterate used it as signature. The last letter in the Hebrew alphabet originally was written as a cross. They called it "taw" which simply means "mark".[1] This leads us to the conclusion that the mark on Cain's forehead and the "taw" of which Ezechiel speaks and the "seal of the Living God" of the Apocalypse, are nothing else but the cross.

The cross upon Cain's forehead is a sign of protection and mercy.[2] It saved the life of the first fratricide and made him God's own property. But it received its deepest meaning when a later and greater fratricide was committed, and Christ who had made Himself one of us was crucified by us, His brothers. Since then it has become a sign of eternal life to all those who, looking at the cross, realize in true compunction of heart that they have killed their Brother. In baptism and confirmation they receive in their souls the "seal of the Living God" which is in very deed the life of the crucified and risen Lord.[3]

The Tree of Life

"And the Lord brought forth of the ground all manner of trees, fair to behold and pleasant to eat of: the tree of life also in the midst of paradise." (*Genesis* 2, 9).

"The Wisdom of God is a true tree of life to all that lay hold upon her." (*Proverbs* 3, 18).

"In the midst of the street, and on both sides of the river, was the tree of life, bearing twelve fruits, yielding its fruits every month, and the leaves of the tree were for the healing of the nations." (*Apocalypse* 22,2).

The Tree of Life

THE tree has always played an important part in folk-lore and myth.[1] It symbolizes the eternal cycle of life and death and resurrection; it is a figure as well as a pledge of community life. In spring the tree puts forth its tender buds and flowers; through the long summer its leafy branches cover both men and beasts with shade and comfort; and in fall, when its work is done and its lifegiving fruits have been plucked from its withering limbs, its sap returns to the earth for the winter to await the resurrection of spring. Families, tribes, empires are likened to trees. The cosmic tree which stands on the top of the mountain of God and upholds the dome of heaven is a symbol of world order.

All this symbolism of the tree has found its fulfillment in Christ. He is foreshadowed in the tree of life which was planted in the midst of paradise, for "the Wisdom of God is a true tree of life to all that lay hold upon her" (*Proverbs* 3, 18). Christ is "the tender twig that is planted on the high mountains of Israel, that shoots forth into branches and becomes a great cedar and all the birds dwell under it" (*Ezechiel*, 17, 22), whilst the "high tree," symbol of the kingdom of this world, shall be cut down (*Ezechiel* 31, 12. *Daniel* 4, 12). Christ, who dies on the cross and rises again is indicated in the rod of Aaron (*Numbers* 17, 8) and in the dry tree which God causes to flourish (*Ezechiel* 17, 24). The risen Christ is the true vine of which we are the branches (*John* 15, 1). He is the tree that grows on the river of the heavenly city, and yields its fruits in all eternity.

The Holy Mountain

"And in the last days the mountain of the house of the Lord shall be prepared on the top of the mountains, and it shall be exalted above the hills, and all nations shall flow unto it." (*Isaias* 2, 2).

"A stone was cut out of the mountain without hands, and it struck the statue upon the feet . . . and broke them in pieces. . . . But the stone that struck the statue, became a great mountain, and filled the whole earth."
(*Daniel* 2, 31/35).

REMOTE and inaccessible, rising high above this earth into the skies in lonely majesty the mountains seem to be the natural thrones of the gods. People of old used to regard this earth as a cosmic mountain, surrounded by the waters of chaos, and surmounted by the abode of the deity.[1]

In Holy Scripture the history of the Holy Mountain begins with man's presumptuous attempt to build the "tower of Babel," a man-made "mountain of God" (*Gen.* 11). But "behold I am against thee, O destroying mountain, . . . and I will stretch out my hand upon thee and roll thee down from the rocks, and will make thee a burnt mountain. And they shall not take of thee a stone for a corner" (*Jeremias* 51, 25). God's mountain is a mountain of His own choosing. He does not choose the "fat Basan" but the small and modest Mount Sion (*Psalm* 67, 17). From this mountain the stone will be cut off which smashes the idol and grows into a mountain that fills the whole earth. The stone is Christ, Who by His death and resurrection has overcome the prince of this world and has become the head of the Mystical Body which, since Pentecost, fills the whole world. The risen Christ and His Mystical Body is the "mountain of God's inheritance, the most firm habitation which God has made" (*Exodus* 15, 17). In this mountain we are planted through baptism. But still we have to pray that we may be able "to reach that mountain which is Christ" (*Feast of St. Catharine of Alexandria, Collect*), till the other mountain "burning with fire is cast into the sea." (*Apoc.* 8, 8).

The Burning Bush

"Now Moses . . . came to the mountain of God, Horeb. And the Lord appeared to him in a flame of fire out of the midst of a bush[1]: and he saw that the bush was on fire and was not burnt. And Moses said: I will go and see this great sight, why the bush is not burnt. And the Lord called him out of the midst of the bush, and said: Moses, Moses. And he answered: Here I am. And he said: Come not nigh hither, put off the shoes from thy feet, for the place whereon thou standest is holy ground. And he said: I am the God of thy father, the God of Abraham, the God of Isaac, and the God of Jacob. . . . I am come down to deliver my people out of the hands of the Egyptians." (*Exodus* 3, 2/8).

AFTER the fall God made the earth bring forth thorns which, since then, have been likened to sinners (*Genesis* 3, 18), good only to be set on fire and burnt to nothing (*II Kings* 23, 7). But when the fire of the divine presence descended upon the thornbush on the Holy Mountain, the thornbush was *not* burnt. Certainly a "great sign" and full of consolation! What else can it mean but that God will be with His people to save them, not to judge them,[2] although they are a stubborn and disloyal people, and He a "devouring fire" (*Deuteron.* 4, 24).

According to the Hebrew text and to the account which St. Stephen gives before the high priests (*Acts* 7, 30) it was the "angel of the Lord" who appeared in the fire. The Fathers see in the mysterious "Angel of the Lord" who so often appears in the earlier parts of the Old Testament, the Son of God, the "Angel of the great counsel" (*cf. St. Augustine, sermo* 7, 3). Therefore they interpret the apparition in the burning bush as a manifestation of the Second Person of the Holy Trinity, revealing Himself as the Saviour of His people.[3] The sign became reality when the Word of God descended upon Mary, and preserving her glorious virginity assumed the "likeness of sinful flesh" (*Rom.* 8, 3).[4] Christ, true God and true man, is the Burning Bush. Not He alone. He had come to cast fire upon the earth (*Luke* 12, 49), the saving fire of His love. On Pentecost it descended upon the apostles. Since then it burns in the thornbush of the Church, till New-Jerusalem descends from heaven of which it is written: "The glory of God lights it up, and the Lamb is the lamp thereof." (*Apoc.* 21, 23).

The Brazen Serpent

"And the Lord said to Moses: Make a brazen serpent and set it up for a sign: whosoever being struck shall look at it, shall live. Moses therefore made a brazen serpent, and set it up for a sign: which when they that were bitten looked upon, they were healed."

(Numbers 21, 8/9)

"No man has ascended into heaven except him who has descended from heaven: the Son of Man who is in heaven. And as Moses lifted up the serpent in the desert, even so must the Son of Man be lifted up, that those who believe in him may not perish, but may have life everlasting." *(John* 3, 13/15).

OF ALL SYMBOLS of Christ in the Old Testament the Brazen Serpent certainly is the most "shocking" one. The serpent, symbol of sin and of Satan (*cf. Genesis* 3, 1; *Apoc.* 12, 9): a picture of Christ! But seen in the light of the crucified Saviour the mysterious sign reveals its meaning. On the cross "He Who knew no sin was made sin for us, so that in Him we might be made the justice of God" (*II Cor.* 5, 21). Not a real serpent, but the brazen *likeness* of it was lifted up in the desert. So did Christ come in the *likeness* of sinful flesh (*Rom.* 8, 3), taking upon Himself the pains of sin, without sin (*Hebr.* 4, 15). As the serpent was lifted up on the pole, so He was lifted up on the cross, and as the likeness of the serpent was made of metal as a lasting memorial, so did the death of the Saviour become a lasting memorial in the Holy Sacrifice of the Mass.

All those who are bitten by the serpents of their sins should turn to the crucified Saviour, to be healed from their wounds. Only one condition they have to fulfill. The Book of Wisdom points to it: "He that turned to the Brazen Serpent was not healed by that which he saw, but by Thee the Saviour of all. . . . For it is Thou, O Lord, that hast power of life and death, and leadest down to the gates of death and bringest back again" (*Wisdom* 16, 8/13). Only those, who, looking at the crucified Saviour, say with the centurian under the cross: "Truly this man was the Son of God," will receive new and everlasting life.

The Star of Jacob

"Balaam the son of Beor, the man whose eyes are open, has said: I shall see him, but not now: I shall behold him, but not nigh: there shall come a star out of Jacob, and a sceptre shall rise out of Israel, and shall strike the chiefs of Moab." (*Numbers* 24, 17).

"Now when Jesus was born in Bethlehem of Juda in the days of Herod the king, behold there came wise men from the east to Jerusalem, saying, Where is he that is born king of the Jews? for we have seen his star in the east, and are come to adore him." (*Matth.* 2,2).

"I, Jesus, am the bright morning star." (*Apoc.* 22, 16).

THE STAR OF JACOB

THE FACT that the course of the celestial bodies influences life on earth led people of old to the belief that the heavenly world of the stars is the archetype and model of the earthly world, and that the stars in their unchangeable course—"dei æterni," as the Greeks used to call them—determine the fate of man.

In the Old Testament the stars are not gods. They are the obedient servants of the Lord of hosts who created them. "They were called and they said: Here we are: and with cheerfulness they have shined forth to Him that made them" (*Baruch* 3, 35). When God laid the corner stone of the earth, "the morning stars sang together, and all the sons of God shouted with joy" (*Job* 38, 7). The stars are symbols of the just who obey God's commands and, therefore, declare His glory.

The king of Babylon is the rebellious star who wants to rule without serving his God. He is overthrown by the creator of heaven and earth, as Isaias says of him: "How art thou fallen from heaven, Lucifer, son of the morning? How art thou fallen to the earth that didst wound the nations?" (*Isaias* 14, 12). Only one star will rise to world domination: the "star of Jacob," the Messias. He is the "morning star," because He was begotten before the day of creation (*Psalm* 109). When He appears here on earth, the "star in the east" rises to announce His birth. He runs His course in perfect obedience, and glorifies His Heavenly Father (*John* 17, 4). When the Last Day dawns, He will be there, "the bright morning-star," and those who have overcome will receive Him (*Apoc.* 2, 28) and He will rise in their hearts. (*II Peter* 1, 19).

The Rod of Jesse

"And there shall come forth a rod out of the root of Jesse, and a flower shall rise up out of his root. And the spirit of the Lord shall rest upon him." (*Isaias* 11, 1).

"Behold the days come, saith the Lord, and I will raise unto David a righteous branch, and a king shall reign and prosper, and shall execute justice and judgment in the earth." (*Jeremias* 23, 5).

"Behold the man whose name is "the Offspring," and he shall grow up out of this place and he shall build the temple of the Lord." (*Zacharias* 6, 12).

"I, Jesus, am the root and the offspring of David."
(*Apoc.* 22, 16).

ONE of the titles which were used for the king in the Ancient East was that of the "Branch" or the "Offspring." It designates the king as the legitimate ruler, the scion of an old family which traces its origins back to the gods.

The Old Testament lives in the expectation of the "Offspring," the Messias, whom God had promised solemnly to David: "I will raise up thy seed after thee ... and I will establish the throne of his kingdom for ever. I will be to him a father, and he shall be to me a son." (*II Kings* 7). This promise became true, when Jesus was born of the seed of David according to the flesh (*Rom.* 1, 3). He was truly the Son of His Heavenly Father from all eternity. His throne was established for ever when God raised Him up from the dead, not to return any more to corruption (*Acts* 13, 34).

This Jesus is the "Rod of Jesse" (*Isaias* 11, 1), the "Root and the Offspring of David" (*Apoc.* 22, 16). He is the *Root* of David, because He is the Eternal Son of God, the Beginning of all things, of Whom it is said: "Thou art my Son, today have I begotten thee" (*Psalm* 2, 7; *Hebrew* 1, 5). He is the *Offspring* of David according to the flesh, as the son of the virgin Mary. Through His resurrection He became the "Lord of the Spirit" (*II Cor.* 3, 18), the flower which breathes the "sweet odor of Christ," the Holy Spirit, into the hearts of the faithful. The symbol of the "rod of Jesse," therefore, expresses the eternal as well as the temporal origin of Christ and His eternal rule as that of the Risen Lord.[1]

The Key of David

"And the key of the house of David will I lay upon his shoulder: and he shall open and none shall shut: and he shall shut, and none shall open." (*Isaias* 22,22).

"And I will give to thee the keys of the kingdom of heaven. And whatsoever thou shalt bind upon earth, it shall be bound also in heaven: and whatsoever thou shalt loose on earth, it shall be loosed also in heaven."
(*Matthew* 16, 19).

"Thus says the Holy one, the True one, He Who has the key of David, He Who opens and no one shuts, and Who shuts and no one opens." (*Apoc.* 3, 7).

H E WHO holds the key of the house wields power over it. When a city surrenders, the keys are brought to the conqueror, not only the keys of the gates, but also the keys of the storehouse and those of the prison house as well.

The "power of the keys" is threefold: over the entrance gate to admit or to exclude, over the prison to punish or to condone, over the storehouse and the treasure to feed and to reward.

Isaias tells us (22, 22) how Eljakim received the "key of the house of David" and, thence, received full power over the royal palace and the whole kingdom as administrator and representative of the king.

Eljakim is an archetype of the Messias, the "offspring of David," to whom is given, at the end of time, full power over the messianic kingdom which was promised to the house of David. The glorified and exalted Christ has received from His Heavenly Father the "key of David" (*Apoc.* 3, 7) with its threefold power. Through His death He has conquered death and possesses "the keys of Death and of Hades" (*Apoc.* 1, 18) to "bring the prisoners out of the prison house, them that sit in darkness and in the shadow of death" (O Antiphon). He has power over the gates of the heavenly Jerusalem. All its citizens are written in the "book of life of the Lamb" (*Apoc.* 21, 27). Finally the risen Christ has the key to the heavenly store house, for, as St. Peter says (*Acts* 2, 33), "exalted by the right hand of God, and receiving from the Father the promise of the Holy Spirit, He has poured forth this Spirit which you see and hear."[1]

The Corner Stone

"The stone which the builders rejected, the same is become the head of the corner. This is the Lord's doing: and it is wonderful in our eyes." (*Psalm* 117, 22/23).

"And Jesus said: What then is this that is written: The stone which the builders rejected, has become the cornerstone? Everyone who falls upon that stone will be broken to pieces, but upon whomever it falls, it will grind him to powder." (*Luke* 20, 17/18).

"You are built upon the foundations of the apostles and the prophets with Christ Jesus Himself as the chief corner stone . . . in Him you are being built together into a dwelling place for God in the Spirit."

(*Ephesians* 2, 20/22).

THE CORNER STONE

STONE is firm and lasting. Builders test their stones selecting the most solid for foundations on which to rear the whole building, for corner stones to hold the walls together, or for headstones which will lock into a single mass the entire structure. Stone likewise offers firm resistance to the thrusts of an enemy; it will crush him upon whom it falls; it will bruise those who fall against it.

God is the "stone of Israel" (*Genesis* 49, 24), because He is a God of truth and His mercies endure forever. His faithfulness towards His people is the firm and precious corner stone which is laid in Sion (*Isaias* 28, 16). In Christ Jesus God's loyalty becomes manifest. He is the corner stone which was rejected in the crucifixion by the leaders of His people, but chosen by God in the resurrection (*Acts* 4, 11). The glorified Christ is the "firm rock," the foundation stone of the Kingdom of God, since our faith and our salvation stand on the resurrection. He is the corner stone, for in Him the two walls of God and humanity, of the Jews and the Gentiles, of the Old and the New Testament are fitted together. He is the headstone[1] of the temple which culminates the whole building and holds it together (*Ephesians* 2, 20). But to those who have no faith Christ will be "a stone of stumbling and a rock of scandal" (*I Peter* 2, 4-8), on the Day of Judgment. On that day the stone will fall down from the mountain to smash the idols and will grow into a rock "higher than the hills, four-square, so that it could hold the whole world." (*Pastor Hermae, similitude IX, ch.* 2,1).

The Sun of Justice

"For behold the day shall come kindled as a furnace: and all the proud, and all that do wickedly shall be stubble: and the day that comes shall set them on fire ... But unto you that fear my name, the Sun of Justice shall arise, and health in his wings." (*Malachias* 4, 1/2).

"And after six days Jesus takes Peter, James and John his brother and brings them up into a high mountain apart: and he was transfigured before them: and his face did shine as the sun." (*Matth.* 17, 1/2).

"And I saw one ... like to the Son of Man ... and His countenance was as the sun shining in its power."

(*Apoc.* 1, 16).

IN ANTIQUITY, when our concept of "nature" as regulated by "laws" was unknown, the sun, the moon and the stars were regarded as "powers." The sun appeared to be a mighty ruler who every morning conquers the powers of darkness and "rejoices as a giant to run the way" (*Psalm* 18). From the height of the skies it gave light and life to the world, and "there is no one that can hide himself from his heat" (*Psalm* 18). The sun was conqueror, ruler and judge.

Christ is "the Sun of Justice." He is God's eternal Wisdom, "the brightness of eternal light and the unspotted mirror of God's majesty" (*Wisdom* 7, 26). His crucifixion is likened to the setting of the sun. He descended into "the lower parts of the earth" (*Ephes.* 4, 9) to bring light to those who were waiting in darkness and in the shadow of death. In His resurrection He became "the dayspring from on high" (*Luke* 1, 79), the bringer of a new age of light, of life and of salvation to His Church which is likened to the moon, receiving its light from the sun. The whole life of the Church and of Christians is turned toward Christ as to the sun. The first day of the week, the "Sunday," is celebrated as the weekly memorial of Christ's resurrection. Churches and altars look in the direction of the rising sun. At baptism the Sun of Justice illumines the hearts of the neophytes so that they sing, together with all Christians: "As the sun is the joy of those who seek the day, so is the Lord my joy because He is my sun."

(*Odes of Solomon*).

Additional Notes

THE SEAL OF THE LIVING GOD

[1] The Hebrew letter "taw" originally had the form of the so-called "Greek cross" which has four equal arms. Some of the Fathers (cf. Epistle of Barnabas 9, 8; Tertullian, *Adv. Marcionem* III, 22) understood the Hebrew sign "taw" of Ezechiel 9, 4 to be the *Greek* letter "taw" or the Latin T and thus were led to the conclusion that the gallows-shaped cross, the so-called "crux commissa," was the kind of cross on which Christ died.

[2] On the mark on Cain's forehead, cf. Bernhard Stade, *Das Kainszeichen, Zeitschrift für Alttestamentliche Wissenschaft* XIV, 1894, p. 250 *et seq.*

[3] The various prototypes of the cross in the Old Testament are enumerated by St. John Damascene *de fide orthodoxa* IV, 11: "A prototype of the precious cross was the tree of life which God had planted in paradise. . . . Jacob clearly described the cross when he blessed his sons with his arms crossed. (*Gen.* 48, 14). The staff of Moses which divided the sea, saved Israel and drowned the Egyptians (*Exod.* 14, 16). The wood that turned the bitter water into sweetness (*Exod.* 15, 25). The rod with which Moses struck the rock (*Exod.* 17, 6). The rod which gave the priesthood to Aaron (*Numbers* 17, 8). The serpent lifted up on the pole (*Numbers* 21, 9,). And what Moses said: 'And thy life shall be as it were hanging before thee' (*Deuteron.* 28, 66) and Isaias: 'I have spread forth my hands all day to an unbelieving people'." (*Isaias* 65, 2).

THE TREE OF LIFE

[1] The most popular survivals of the sacred tree in our days are the Maypole and the Christmas tree. In spring, on the first of May, during Whitsuntide or even on Midsummer Day it was and still is the custom in many parts of the Old and of the New World to go out to the woods, cut down a tree and bring

it into the village, where it is set up amid general rejoicings. The intention of these customs is to bring home to the village, and to each house, the blessings of the season which are embodied in the tree (*cf.* J. G. Frazer, *The Golden Bough,* abridged ed., New York, 1942, p. 120 ff). The blessing of the branches on Palm Sunday gives a Christian meaning to the old pagan custom.

The Christmas tree, in its present form, is of comparatively recent origin. It is an old medieval tradition that trees and flowers blossomed on Christmas night. But it was only after the Reformation that the Protestants, especially in Northern Germany, patronized the Christmas tree to counteract the Catholic custom of having representations of the crib in the homes. It was introduced into France and England in 1840 only, by Princess Helena of Mecklenburg. (*cf.* Tiele, *Yule and Christmas,* London, 1899).

THE HOLY MOUNTAIN

[1] According to ideas current in the ancient East the earth was a great hollow mountain, containing the cavernous regions of darkness — the "deep pit," the realm of the dead. The waters of the deep are kept from flooding this earth by a great rock which seals its top. Here is the entrance to the world below, the "gates of hell" (*cf. Matth.* 16, 18). Every country is a world in miniature and has its Holy Mountain, its "navel" or link with the celestial world (*cf.* A. Jeremias, *The Old Testament in the Light of the Ancient East,* 1911, vol. I, p. 54). On the Forum in Rome we can see up to this day the place of the "omphalos" (navel) or center of the Roman Empire from which the legions set out to conquer the world. In similar fashion the Jews held that "the land of Israel is in the heart of the world, Jerusalem is in the heart of the land, the temple is in the heart of Jerusalem, and the ark of the covenant is in the midst of the temple. Next to the ark is the keystone of the world." (bin Gorion, *Die Sagen der Juden,* 1927, p. 182).

Usually close by the central rock a well or spring flowed up from the floodwaters below which the great rock held back. By the "omphalos" on the Roman Forum is Lake Juturna which the Romans held to be the entrance to Hades. Similarly a stream issued from the temple mount in Jerusalem. "There is a river, the streams whereof shall make glad the city of God, the holy place of the tabernacles of the most High" (*Psalm* 45, 4). This river prefigures the waters of grace which, in the messianic times issue forth from the Risen Lord, God's Holy Mountain of the New Covenant (*Apoc.* 22, 1).

THE BURNING BUSH

[1] The Hebrew "Sené" is a thornbush, probably a kind of hawthorn. The Vulgate translates "rubus" — bramble bush.

[2] That the burning bush is a manifestation of God's saving love has been pointed out by Jewish interpreters also. We quote Ginsberg, *Legends of the Jews*, vol. II, p. 304: "God's choosing to dwell in the stunted thornbush conveyed the knowledge to Moses that He suffers along with Israel. Furthermore Moses was taught that there is nothing in nature, not even the insignificant and despised thornbush, that can exist without the presence of the Shekinah (the cloud of God's glory, *cf. Luke* 9, 34). Besides, the thornbush may be taken as a symbol of Israel in several respects. As the thornbush is the lowliest of all the species of trees, so the condition of Israel in exile is the lowliest as compared with that of all other nations. . . . Further in order to give Moses an illustration of His modesty God descended from the exalted heaven and spake to him from a lowly thornbush instead of the summit of a lofty mountain or at the top of a stately cedar tree."
Of the Fathers, St. Augustine has most fully explained the symbolism of the burning bush in sermo VI and VIII. *He*, however, explains the thornbush as a symbol of the Jewish people in their sinfulness and stubbornness.

[3] The apparition in the bush has been referred to as the Second Person of The Holy Trinity in the antiphon: "O Adonai and Leader of the house of Israel, who appearedst in the bush to Moses in a flame of fire and gavest him the law on Sinai: come and redeem us with an outstretched arm."

[4] A later age applied the symbol of the burning bush to Our Lady, as we have it in the Antiphon of the Feast of the Circumcision: "In the Bush which Moses saw unconsumed, we acknowledge the preservation of thy glorious virginity: holy Mother of God, intercede for thy children."

THE BRAZEN SERPENT

In the text the interpretation follows that of St. Augustine.
sermo 294, opera ed. Migne V, 1342
enarr. in psalmos 118, sermo 26, 4, opera IV, 1578

A brief summary of his interpretation is given in *De Civitate Dei*, book X, chapter 8: "The deadly serpent's bites, sent in just punishment of sin, were healed by looking at the lifted brazen serpent, so that not only were the tormented people healed, but a symbol of the crucifixion of death set before them in this destruction of death by death."

THE ROD OF JESSE

1 St. Jerome, in his commentary to Isaias ch. 11, mentions the fact that a change has taken place in the interpretation of the symbolism of the "Rod of Jesse." The Jews, following the original Hebrew text of Isaias 11, 1 which speaks of the "shoot" that comes forth out of the "stump" of Jesse, apply it to the Messiah. The Christians follow the Vulgate translation of the same verse: "There shall come forth a *stem* out of the root of Jesse, and a *flower* shall rise up out of his root." They then refer the "stem" to Mary, the mother of the Messiah, and the "flower" to Christ. As an example we quote St. Ambrose, *de benedictionibus Patriarcharum*, n. 19: "The root is the Jewish people (familia Judaeorum), the stem is Mary, the flower of Mary is Christ." One may compare the Final Antiphon of the Blessed Virgin: "Queen of the heavens, we hail thee . . . Thou the root, thou the door, whence the world's true light is risen."

THE KEY OF DAVID

1 At Caesarea Philippi Christ gave the "power of the keys" to St. Peter: "And I will give thee the keys of the kingdom of heaven; and whatever thou shalt bind on earth shall be bound in heaven, and whatever thou shalt loose on earth shall be loosed in heaven" (*Matth.* 16, 19). From what has been said about the symbolism of the key it follows that Christ's promise to St. Peter is not restricted to signify the power to forgive sins but has to be taken in the fuller meaning of the gift of authority over the Church. It includes especially the

power of teaching, the "key of knowledge" (*cf. Luke* 11, 52).

The precise significance of the term was analyzed in various ways by the Scholastic theologians, till Saurez gave the now universally accepted interpretation that the "power of the keys" includes: [a] the power of order, namely, power exercised in regard to sacrifice and sacrament; [b] the power of jurisdiction; and [c] the power to define in questions of faith and morals.

THE CORNER STONE

[1] The controversy over the term "chief corner stone," whether it means "foundation stone" or "key stone" (*cf.* J. Jeremias, *Der Eckstein*, Angelos I, 1925, p. 65 ff. *Theologisches Woerterbuch zum Neuen Testament*, I, 792/793, A. K. Coomaraswamy, *Eckstein*, Speculum XIV, 1939, pp. 66-72) will probably not be solved by saying that Christ is exclusively one or the other. Christ, fully understood, is both. He is the foundation stone, "for other foundation no man can lay but that which is laid, which is Christ Jesus" (*I Cor.* 3, 11). As head of the Mystical Body, He is the key stone.

Actually, the Hebrew expression "rosch pinnah"—still surviving in our word "pinnacle"—which we rather vaguely translate "head of the corner" or "chief corner stone," points more to a coping or cap stone than to a foundation or corner stone (*cf. Zacharias* 4, 7 and *Job* 38, 6).

Cynewulf, in his poem *Christ,* interpreting the O Antiphon "O King of nations and their Desired, the Corner stone who makest both one . . ." best expresses the key stone idea:

> "Thou art the wall stone   that the workers once
> threw out from the work,   well it becomes Thee
> that Thou be head   of a mighty hall
> and weld together   its wide walls
> in fast union,   flint unbreakable,
> that throughout earth's dwelling   all that have eyes
> may wonder evermore,   O Lord of Glory."
>
> (*cf.* M. Williams, *Word Hoard*, 1940, p. 224).

THE SUN OF JUSTICE

[1] On Christ as "the Sun of Justice" an abundance of material is to be found in Fr. J. Doelger, *Sol Solutis*, Muenster i.W., 1925.

The most beautiful expression of Christ as the Sun is found in the Hymn for Lauds on Monday:

> Thou brightness of the Father's ray,
> True Light of light and Day of day,
> Light's Fountain and eternal Spring,
> Thou Morn the morn illumining!
> Glide in, thou very Sun divine
> With everlasting brightness shine:
> and shed abroad on every sense
> The Spirit's light and influence.

THE COVER SYMBOL

The symbol on the cover is taken from the rood-screen in the chapel of St. Paul's Priory. The sign in the center of the wreath is composed of the Greek letters Chi and Rho, the first two letters of the word "Christos" which is the Greek translation of the Hebrew "Messiah," the "Anointed One." The wreath is a symbol of the new life which Christ gives us through His sacraments and His words. The two doves picking at the wreath signify the faithful who, in baptism, have received the Holy Spirit and therefore are likened to birds which master the air with their wings. They stand on the cross, because it is through the death of Christ that they have received life. The A and O are the first and the last letter of the Greek alphabet. They stand for eternity and universality: "world without end." In the power of the Spirit do the faithful take part in the eternal life that emanates from Christ.

VAN VECHTEN PRESS, METUCHEN, N. J.